Life in the Colonies

BY
CINDY BARDEN

COPYRIGHT © 2001 Mark Twain Media, Inc.

ISBN   10-digit: 1-58037-175-2
         13-digit: 978-1-58037-175-9

Printing No. CD-1396

Mark Twain Media, Inc., Publishers
Distributed by Carson-Dellosa Publishing Company, Inc.

Table of Contents

1	About the American History Series	32	Many Skills Needed
2	Time Line of *Life in the Colonies*	33	Livestock
3	Exploring a New World	34	Trading for Goods and Services
4	Colonizing the New World	35	The Importance of Water
5	Why Did People Become Colonists?	36	Millers
6	Moving to the Colonies	37	The Importance of Sawmills
7	Where Were the First Colonies?	38	Coopers
8	Building a Log Cabin	39	Cabinetmakers
9	Living in a Log Cabin	40	Wheelwrights
10	The Kitchen—The Heart of the Colonial Home	41	Blacksmiths
		42	Pewterers and Silversmiths
11	Baking Bread	43	Tinsmiths
12	Making Butter	44	Leatherworkers
13	Preserving Food	45	Papermakers
14	Colonial Tools	46	Printers
15	Learning About New Foods	47	Apprentices
16	What's for Dinner?	48	The Role of Colonial Women
17	The First Thanksgiving	49	Colonists Wanted
18	Recycling Was a Way of Life	50	Life in a Colonial Village
19	Candlemaking	51	Community Spirit
20	Soapmaking	52	Shopping at the General Store
21	Dyeing for Color	53	Colonial Education
22	Colonial Quilts	54	Make a Quill Pen
23	From Wool to Clothing	55	Rules of Civility & Decent Behaviour in Company and Conversation
24	Weaving		
25	Make a Sampler	56	Interview a Colonist
26	Spice Up Your Life	57	Colonial Scavenger Hunt
27	Making Watertight Containers	58	Colonial Word Search
28	Tidbits of Colonial Trivia	59	Report on a Colonist
29	Make a Whirligig	60	Suggested Reading
30	Cornhusk Dolls	61	Answer Keys
31	Nine Men's Morris		

About the American History Series

Welcome to *Life in the Colonies,* one of the books in the Mark Twain Media, Inc., American History series for students in grades four to seven.

The activity books in this series are designed as stand-alone material for classrooms and home-schoolers or as supplemental material to enhance your history curriculum. Students can be encouraged to use the books as independent study units to improve their understanding of historical events and people.

Each book provides challenging activities that enable students to explore history, geography, and social studies topics. The activities provide research opportunities and promote critical reading, thinking, and writing skills. As students learn about the customs, crafts, and occupations of colonial people, they will draw conclusions; write opinions; compare and contrast historical events, people, and places; analyze cause and effect; and improve mapping skills. Students will also have the opportunity to apply what they learn to their own lives through reflection, creative writing, and hands-on activities.

Students can further increase their knowledge and understanding of historical events by using reference sources at the library and on the Internet. Students may need assistance to learn how to use search engines and discover appropriate websites.

Titles of books for additional reading appropriate to the subject matter at this grade level are included in each book.

Although many of the questions are open-ended, an answer key is included at the back of the book for questions with specific answers.

Share a journey through history with your students as you explore the books in the Mark Twain Media, Inc., American History series:

Discovering and Exploring the Americas
Life in the Colonies
The American Revolution
The Lewis and Clark Expedition
The Westward Movement
The California Gold Rush
The Oregon and Sante Fe Trails
Slavery in the United States
The American Civil War
Abraham Lincoln and His Times
The Reconstruction Era
Industrialization in America
The Roaring Twenties and Great Depression
World War II and the Post-War Years
America in the 1960s and 1970s
America in the 1980s and 1990s

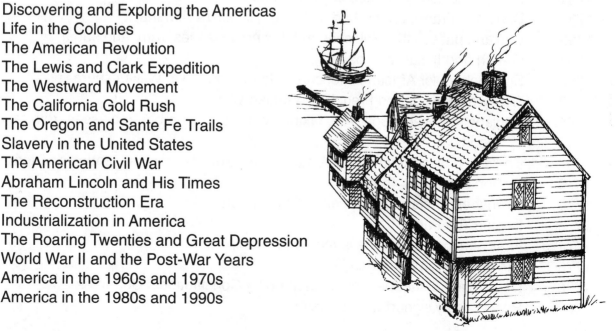

Time Line of *Life in the Colonies*

1565	St. Augustine, Florida, founded by Pedro Menendez
1584	Sir Walter Raleigh landed on Roanoke Island
1607	Jamestown, Virginia, colony founded
1613	Dutch trading post established on Manhattan
1619	First Africans brought to the Americas as indentured servants
1620	Pilgrims landed and formed Plymouth colony
1624	Dutch colonists arrived in New Netherlands
1626	Peter Minuit bought the island of Manhattan and named it New Amsterdam
1630	Boston, Massachusetts, founded by John Winthrop
1633	First public school opened in America
1634	Catholic colony founded in Maryland
1636	Providence, Rhode Island, founded by Roger Williams
1636	Harvard College founded in Boston
1638	Anne Hutchinson banished from Massachusetts for religious reasons
1638	First Swedish settlers arrived at Fort Christina, Delaware
1640	First book printed in America: *Bay Psalm Book*
1652	Rhode Island declared slavery illegal
1673	Jacques Marquette and Louis Joliet explore the Mississippi River
1682	Robert La Salle claimed area along the Mississippi River for France; named it Louisiana
1683	Quaker colony founded in Pennsylvania by William Penn
1692	Witchcraft trials in Salem, Massachusetts
1700	Boston (population 7,000) became largest colonial city
1718	New Orleans founded by the French
1731	First public library opened in Philadelphia
1732	Benjamin Franklin published first *Poor Richard's Almanack*
1733	England passed the Molasses Act, taxing molasses, rum, and sugar
1754	French and Indian War began
1760	Bray School for African-American children opened in Williamsburg
1763	Treaty of Paris ended French and Indian War
1764	England imposed Sugar Act, taxing colonists on lumber, molasses, rum, and other foods
1767	England passed Townshend Acts, taxing colonists on glass, paper, and tea
1770	Boston Massacre
1770	Townshend Acts repealed, except tax on tea
1773	Boston Tea Party
1774	First Continental Congress met in Philadelphia
1775	Revolutionary War began
1776	Declaration of Independence adopted by Constitutional Congress
1783	Peace treaty signed with England

Name: _____ Date: _____

Exploring a New World

After Columbus made his first voyage to the New World in 1492, other explorers from Spain, Italy, France, England, and the Netherlands followed. They all searched for a water route to the Far East, a land rich in silks and spices.

When he landed at San Salvador, Columbus thought he had reached islands near China or India. At that time, no one realized that the continents of North and South America even existed.

By the mid 1500s, explorers had discovered that North and South America were not part of Asia, but a whole New World. Then they faced a new challenge: how to get around the continents to where they really wanted to go.

They tried sailing around South America to reach the East. That worked, but it was a long way around.

Explorers searched for a water passage through the middle of the continents but found none. They tried to sail north across the Arctic Ocean but were stopped by ice floes. They searched for inland waterways across North America. For over two centuries, explorers tried in vain to find a route that didn't exist.

The king of Spain sent armies to Central and South America in the 1500s to conquer, explore, and search for gold and silver. Some of the soldiers decided to stay and establish small colonies in Central and South America and on the islands offshore.

French fisherman regularly sailed to the coast of Newfoundland in the 1500s where fish were plentiful. They stayed a few months and then returned home with their catches. A few French fur traders also realized they could profit from the new land.

1. Navigators knew the earth was round, but they didn't realize how large it was. Look at a world map. If North and South America didn't exist, would it have been possible to sail west from England to reach China and India?

   _____

2. Who was the first explorer to sail around South America to India?

   _____

3. Although people found little gold or silver in North America, the continent had many other valuable resources. What resources did they find?

   _____

   _____

   _____

   _____

Name: _____ Date: _____

Colonizing the New World

New Spain: Spain was the first European nation to send colonists to the New World. The first Spanish colonies were in Cuba, Puerto Rico, Mexico, and South America. Explorers searched for gold and silver, items that helped make Spain a major power in Europe for over 100 years. St. Augustine, Florida, settled in 1565, was the first permanent European colony in North America.

1. Use reference sources: Who founded St. Augustine?_____

New France: Although the French were the first to explore the northern part of North America extensively, they were more interested in the fishing banks off the coast of Newfoundland and furs obtained by trade with the Native Americans. The first permanent French colony in North America was Quebec, founded by Samuel de Champlain in 1608 as a trading post.

2. Use reference sources: What did the words *canada* and *quebec* mean to the Native Americans who lived there?

    canada means _____

    quebec means _____

New England: Although England was rather a latecomer to colonization, that country sent more people (about 400,000) and established more permanent agricultural communities than any other European nation during the seventeenth century. Few English explorers or adventurers had visited North or South America prior to the settlement of Jamestown in 1607. The two major reasons for migrating from England to the New World were religious freedom and acquisition of land.

New Netherlands: Although the Dutch established a string of strong agricultural settlements in the New York area, those settlements were eventually taken over by the English.

New Sweden: The first Swedish colony was founded at Fort Christina, Delaware, in 1638. That and other Swedish colonies were taken over by the Dutch in 1655 and finally by England in 1664.

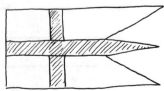

3. Use reference sources: What city in Delaware was once the site of Fort Christina?

_____

Name: _____   Date: _____

Why Did People Become Colonists?

People left their homes to travel to a new, unknown land for many reasons. Some sought adventure and riches. Some left because they were not allowed to practice their religions. Others did not like the way the government was run. Some were poor and wanted a chance to own land and have a better life. They were looking for a brighter future for themselves and their families.

People from every social class, religion, and occupation immigrated to the colonies. Doctors, merchants, business people, and lawyers became colonists. So did craftsmen, fur trappers, soldiers, and farmers. They came alone or with friends and families.

Most of the early colonists were from Europe, mainly England, France, Scotland, Sweden, Spain, Germany, Ireland, and the Netherlands.

No matter what country they were from, what their occupation had been, or where in the colonies they settled, the first priority of colonists would have been to survive. To do that, they needed food and shelter.

1. List ten things that colonists would have had to do within a short time after arriving in America.

_____

_____

_____

_____

_____

_____

_____

_____

_____

_____

2. Number the items in your list from 1 to 10 in the order you think is most important.

5

Name: _____ Date: _____

Moving to the Colonies

Great news! Your family will be sailing to the New World to begin a new life. How exciting! But wait. What will you need when you get there? Where will you get your clothes, food, and furniture? Where will you live? There are many unknowns.

The captain of the ship said you should pack everything you need and be at the dock in one week. Your family includes your mother, father, younger sister, older brother, and yourself. You can take whatever you think you will need. However, there isn't much room on board the ship. Your family may bring only two large trunks (about 4' long, 3' wide, and 3' high) and the clothing you will wear.

You know that there are great forests for wood in the New World, good land for planting, and plenty of fresh water. So ... what do you really need?

1. Make a list of all the items you think you will need to build a house and start a new life. Remember, everything on your list must fit in the two trunks.

Name: _____   Date: _____

Where Were the First Colonies?

By the mid 1700s, there were many colonies along the eastern coast of what later became the United States.

Use an atlas or other reference sources. Label these cities on the map.

Albany	Baltimore	Boston	Charles Town (Charleston)
Hartford	New York	Norfolk	Philadelphia
Plymouth	Portsmouth	Providence	Saint Augustine
Salem	Savannah	Williamsburg	

1. _____

2. _____

3. _____

4. _____

5. _____

6. _____

7. _____

8. _____

9. _____

10. _____

11. _____

12. _____

13. _____

14. _____

15. _____

Name: _____ Date: _____

Building a Log Cabin

Many of the first homes in the colonies were log cabins consisting of one room. Sometimes the builders added a low-ceilinged loft over one section as a sleeping area for the children. The reason early log cabins were not very large was because cutting down trees with an ax, stripping off the branches, and assembling the log cabin was a lot of work. The larger the cabin and the higher the walls, the more logs they needed.

A fireplace provided heat, light, and a place to cook. A hole in the roof allowed the smoke to escape. Log cabin roofs were made of tree bark, saplings, or hollow logs. The floors were simply dirt. Windows and doors might be a blanket or animal hide stretched to block cold air.

1. If each log were approximately one foot in diameter and 16 feet long, how many logs would you need to build a 16 x 16 foot log cabin, 7 feet high? _____

2. Why do you think people did not make the doors and windows in a log cabin very big?

_____

_____

_____

Furniture was simple and often served more than one purpose. Beds could be used as places to sit during the day. Instead of closets, shelves and wooden pegs held most of the family's possessions. Log cabins did not have electricity or indoor plumbing. People carried water from a spring or well in buckets for cooking, cleaning, washing clothes, and bathing. As a result, bathing was considered a luxury. Unless it was warm enough outside to bathe in a spring or lake, all bath water not only had to be carried to the house, but it also had to be heated in kettles over the fireplace. Instead of a toilet, people used an outhouse.

People today take many conveniences for granted, like hot running water, electricity, and indoor plumbing. We have ovens, microwaves, refrigerators, TV's, computers, cars, furnaces, fans, and air conditioners.

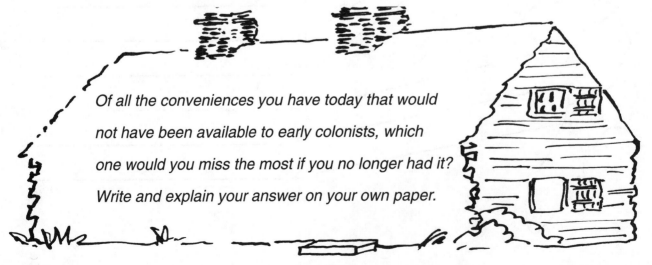

Of all the conveniences you have today that would not have been available to early colonists, which one would you miss the most if you no longer had it? Write and explain your answer on your own paper.

Name: _____ Date: _____

Living in a Log Cabin

Rope off an area 16' by 20' in the gym or outside. This was the approximate size of most early log cabins and represents the total living space for an entire family and all their possessions.

1. How many people can comfortably sit inside this area? _____

2. How would you feel about living in a house this size with two parents, a brother, and a sister?

   _____

   _____

   _____

3. What problems do you think would be common for families living in log cabins?

   _____

   _____

   _____

   _____

4. What do you think would be the biggest disadvantage of living in a log cabin? Explain your answer.

   _____

   _____

   _____

   _____

5. Have you ever heard the expression "cabin fever"? What do you think it means when people say they have cabin fever?

   _____

   _____

   _____

   _____

6. On graph paper, draw a rectangle 8" by 10". This represents the floor plan of a log cabin. Each inch equals two feet. Use this scale to show the location of doors, windows, and the fireplace on the floor plan. Use the same scale to draw furniture a family would have needed, like tables, chairs, beds, etc.

Name: _____ Date: _____

The Kitchen—The Heart of the Colonial Home

Colonists spent much of the time in their kitchens. The large fireplace used for cooking and baking made the kitchen the warmest room in the house. Even when they had houses with several rooms, people often slept in the kitchen in cold weather, gathered there with friends, did their homework, read, sewed, and played games there. The fireplace also provided a source of light.

If you could travel back in time to a colonial kitchen, the first thing you would notice is how different it is from your kitchen.

1. List items in your kitchen that wouldn't have been found in a colonial kitchen. (Remember, electricity and indoor plumbing hadn't been invented yet.) Example: microwave

   _____

   _____

   _____

   _____

   _____

   _____

2. List items that could probably be found in both a modern and colonial kitchen. Example: salt

   _____

   _____

   _____

   _____

   _____

3. Besides cooking and eating, what else do you and your family like to do in your kitchen?

   _____

   _____

   _____

   _____

Name: _____ Date: _____

Baking Bread

Baking bread was a job usually done once a week by colonial women. To bake enough bread for a family took a lot of time and work. Loaves of homemade bread were also given as gifts to friends or neighbors.

To bake bread, women mixed the ingredients in large bowls. It takes about four cups of flour for one loaf of bread. Imagine the size of the bowl needed to mix the ingredients for 10 loaves of bread!

The ingredients needed for baking bread depended on the recipe used. Flour, water, salt, and yeast were the main ingredients.

After mixing the ingredients with a wooden spoon, they formed the dough into a ball and let it "rest" for a few minutes. Then they kneaded the dough.

Kneading dough is hard work. After kneading the dough, they covered it and let it rise in a warm place until it doubled in size (1–2 hours). Then they punched it down, formed it into loaves, and placed the dough in pans to rise again (1–2 hours).

Finally, the bread was ready to bake. Of course, that meant the baker had to gather wood and start a fire in the baking oven so it would be hot enough at the right time. Another 30 to 45 minutes in the oven, and the family would have fresh bread for dinner.

Today, many people use bread machines to bake fresh bread. The process is much simpler. Pour water, bread mix, and yeast into the pan. Plug in the machine, and set the timer. Wait about three hours, and the bread is ready.

1. How much flour would they need for 10 loaves of bread?

   _____

2. Use a dictionary to define *knead.*

   _____

   _____

3. Have you ever eaten freshly made bread?

   _____

4. Compare the smell and taste of fresh bread to store-bought loaves.

   _____

   _____

   _____

   _____

   _____

Name: _____ Date: _____

Making Butter

When colonists ran out of butter, they didn't drive to the store and buy a couple of pounds. If they wanted butter, they either had to make it themselves or buy it from someone else in the colony.

Those who were lucky enough to have a cow were able to enjoy fresh butter, if they were willing to work a bit. Each day, a portion of the milk was set aside. When the creamy portion of the milk rose to the top, it was skimmed off and used to make butter.

Churning butter was a job often done by women or children. First, they poured fresh cream into a butter churn. Then they pushed the handle, called a dasher, up and down. Eventually, the cream turned into butter and buttermilk.

If you have a butter churn, you can make butter the old-fashioned way. If not, try this method.

1. Pour 1 cup of room-temperature whipping cream into a clear plastic container with a tight-fitting lid.

2. Add 3 or 4 well-washed marbles and close tightly.

3. Shake the jar continuously until butter forms. You may want to work with a partner or two, so your arms don't get tired. Record how long it takes.

   _____

4. When butter forms, pour off the liquid into a measuring cup and record the amount.

   _____

   This is buttermilk, which is very delicious. Cool the liquid, and enjoy its rich, creamy taste.

5. You can mix a little salt with the butter, and then put it into the refrigerator to cool and harden.

   How much butter did you make?_____

6. Compare the taste of the butter you made with what you get from a grocery store. Which do you like better? Why?_____

   _____

7. If you had no other way to get butter than to churn it yourself, do you think it would be worth all the work? Why or why not? _____

   _____

   _____

   _____

Name: _____ Date: _____

Preserving Food

The colonists faced many challenges in the New World. One of those challenges was to preserve fruits, vegetables, and meat. Without refrigeration, food spoiled quickly, especially in warm weather. The colonists used several methods to preserve food.

Root cellars kept fruits and vegetables cool during the rest of the year without freezing in winter. Food could also be stored inside crocks in a stream or well to keep it cool in summer.

Meat and fish kept longer when smoked—cooked slowly over a fire.

The colonists made jams, preserves, and jellies from berries and other fruit.

Some types of fruit, vegetables, herbs, meat, and fish could be dried in the sun for several days during the summer and stored for use in winter. People still eat dried beef. Raisins are dried grapes. Several types of snack foods include dried fruit.

Pickling was another way to preserve foods like cucumbers, onions, beets, and cabbages. When cabbage is pickled, it becomes sauerkraut.

1. Have you ever eaten smoked meat or fish? _____

2. Describe how it tasted. _____

   _____

3. What type of jam is your favorite? _____

4. What pickled food do you like best? _____

Here's Your Challenge: Preserve an ice cube for 24 hours.

You can use any method or materials that would have been available to the colonists. (If it's winter, putting it outside is not an option. That's too easy.)

5. Describe the method you used: _____

   _____

   _____

   _____

6. About how much of your ice cube was left after 24 hours? _____

7. What else could you have done to preserve your ice cube? _____

   _____

   _____

   _____

   _____

Name: _____ Date: _____

Colonial Tools

Match the descriptions of the tools with the illustrations.

____ 1. A frying pan with legs and a long handle was called a **spider**.

A.

____ 2. Hot coals were put inside this **iron**. When hot, women used it to smooth wrinkles from clothes.

B.

____ 3. To warm a cold bed at night, colonists filled a **warming pan** with hot coals and moved it between the covers.

C.

____ 4. A **goffer** was used to iron bows and frills on hats and collars.

D.

____ 5. Farmers used a long-handled **hay fork** to gather up straw or hay.

E.

____ 6. Metalworkers used **tongs** to hold hot metal.

F.

____ 7. Woodworkers used a **drawknife** to shape wood by shaving off thin layers.

____ 8. Women used a **hackle** to comb knots from wool and make long threads.

G.

____ 9. Colonists placed a **ruggle** behind a wagon wheel to keep the wagon from rolling away.

H.

____ 10. To clean carpets, people used a **rug beater**.

I.

J.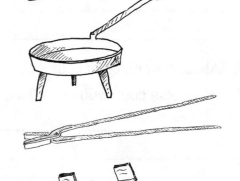

Name: _____ Date: _____

Learning About New Foods

When the colonists arrived, they learned to grow and eat many new foods. Some crops like corn, potatoes, and squash grew only in the New World.

1. Use reference sources. List other foods the colonists learned to eat from Native Americans.

_____

_____

_____

Corn was one of the most important crops colonists learned to grow. Corn on the cob could be roasted or boiled. Shelled corn was ground to make corn cakes or corn mush. Corn husks were used to stuff mattresses, make dolls, and were braided for mats. But best of all, corn could be popped.

Long before the colonists arrived, Native Americans enjoyed fresh, hot popcorn. They introduced this treat to early colonists. Many believe it was one of the foods eaten at the first Thanksgiving in 1621.

Although most varieties of corn look similar, only one type pops. What makes it pop? Actually—water. In fact, each kernel explodes when the small amount of moisture inside is heated. The heat produces steam, and the pressure of the steam inside the corn causes the outside to burst open.

At first people cooked popcorn over glowing coals, but most of the kernels burned. They found they could lay stones on a hot fire and place the kernels on top of the stones to heat them. Fewer kernels burnt, but people were kept quite busy chasing the exploding kernels!

Later, people invented a wire basket to hold the kernels and the popped corn as they cooked it over an open fire. Popping corn in a closed kettle in oil became the standard method for over 100 years. Today, many people enjoy the quickness and convenience of microwave popcorn.

2. Draw a cartoon showing what it might have been like to make popcorn by placing the kernels on stones on a hot fire.

Name: _____ Date: _____

What's for Dinner?

The colonists ate many of the same foods we do today, such as bread, potatoes, beef, ham, turkey, chicken, carrots, corn, and peas. They also ate foods that aren't so common anymore, like squirrel pie and possum stew.

1. List six things colonists could have eaten if they had a cow for milking, chickens that laid eggs, and grain to make flour.

   _____ _____

   _____ _____

   _____ _____

2. List six animals colonists might have hunted or trapped for food.

   _____ _____

   _____ _____

   _____ _____

3. List six other foods colonists might have been able to find in the woods or growing wild.

   _____ _____ _____

   _____ _____ _____

4. List six vegetables colonists may have grown in a garden.

   _____ _____ _____

   _____ _____ _____

5. Using only foods available to colonists, write a menu for three meals and a snack.

   Breakfast: _____

   _____

   _____

   Lunch: _____

   _____

   _____

   Supper: _____

   _____

   _____

   Snack: _____

   _____

Name: _____ Date: _____

The First Thanksgiving

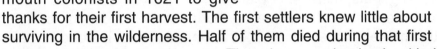

Giving thanks for a bountiful harvest began long before the Pilgrims landed in the New World. The ancient Egyptians, Chinese, Greeks, and Romans all held fall festivals. People in Europe enjoyed feasting, dancing, and playing games at harvest festivals following the grain harvest.

The first American Thanksgiving, three days of prayer and feasting, was celebrated by the Plymouth colonists in 1621 to give thanks for their first harvest. The first settlers knew little about surviving in the wilderness. Half of them died during that first terrible winter in Massachusetts. The others survived only with the assistance of Native Americans.

When the Pilgrims planned their first thanksgiving festival, they prepared food for themselves and their ten expected guests. According to legend, nearly 90 Native Americans arrived. However, Chief Massasoit's hunters brought venison, insuring plenty of food for all.

The date of this thanksgiving festival is unknown, as are many details of what they did and ate. The menu probably included wild turkey, corn, fish, fruit, and venison. The next year the harvest was poor. A second thanksgiving festival wasn't held until 1623.

The custom of holding a thanksgiving festival spread as the colonies grew, but no single date was set. Some places celebrated in October, some in November. Even within the same settlement, the date changed from year to year.

President George Washington proclaimed November 26, 1789, as the first national Thanksgiving holiday, but various communities continued to celebrate Thanksgiving on different days.

In 1863, Sarah Hale persuaded President Abraham Lincoln to declare Thanksgiving as an annual national holiday held on the last Thursday in November. Many people objected when Franklin D. Roosevelt moved Thanksgiving to the third Thursday in November in 1939, to give people more time for Christmas shopping. Of the 48 states, 23 continued to observe the fourth Thursday and 23 celebrated on the earlier date. Two states, Texas and Colorado, celebrated Thanksgiving on both days. In 1941, Congress changed the date back to the fourth Thursday, and there it has remained.

1. On another sheet of paper, write a dialogue that might have taken place on the first Thanksgiving between a pilgrim and a Native American guest.

Name: _____ Date: _____

Recycling Was a Way of Life

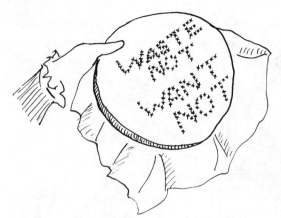

This old saying was very much a part of daily colonial life. Little was wasted. At the end of the week, the colonists didn't set several plastic bags of garbage out to the street. In fact, they had very little garbage.

Colonists said that when they butchered a pig, they used everything except the oink. Besides ham, bacon, pork chops, and roast, people ate pickled pigs' feet, used the skin to make a soft leather, the fat to make tallow, the intestines to make sausage casings, and the bristles to make hair brushes.

The hides of cows, oxen, goats, and other animals were also used to make leather. Furs from some animals were cured to make clothing, hats, mittens, or blankets.

Food scraps and eggshells were fed to the animals or buried in the garden for fertilizer.

Old clothing was reused to make another garment, sewn into quilts, or braided to make rag rugs.

Corn husks were used to make dolls, as stuffing for mattresses, and were braided into baskets or floor mats.

Flour sacks were made into clothing, dish towels, or curtains.

Animal fat and grease were used to make soap and candles. Ashes were also an ingredient in soapmaking.

Pillows and mattresses were stuffed with chicken, duck, and goose feathers. Feathers were used for quill pens.

When you consider how much they recycled or reused, you can understand why the colonists had little garbage at the end of a week.

1. Does your family recycle as well as the colonists did?

    _____

2. List ways you and your family reuse and recycle at home.

    _____

    _____

    _____

    _____

    _____

Name: _____ Date: _____

Candlemaking

Without electricity, colonists relied on firelight, candles, and lanterns as sources of light. They made candles by dipping a wick made of flax or cotton fibers into melted wax or fat, removing it, and letting it cool. The hot wax adhered to the wick and became hard when it cooled. Candles were made thicker by dipping them into the melted wax several times.

Imagine what a candle made from animal fat would smell like when it burned! Herbs, spices, or dried flower petals could be added when candles were made to make them smell better. The most expensive candles were made from beeswax.

1. Read one page of a book by candlelight. Make sure that is the only source of light in the room. Describe the experience.

_____

_____

_____

_____

_____

Did You Know? The nursery rhyme "Jack Be Nimble" is based on a game children played while their parents made candles. After dipping candles, colonial women hung them from two long horizontal sticks to allow them to harden and cool. These sticks, and not the candles themselves, were the "candlesticks" Jack jumped over.

2. Write a short rhyme similar to Jack Be Nimble, based on any aspect of colonial life.

_____

_____

_____

_____

_____

_____

_____

Name: _____ Date: _____

Soapmaking

Bathing with soap and water and washing clothes were not items high on the list of priorities for the colonists. It wasn't uncommon for people to wear the same clothes every day for a month or more and bathe even less frequently.

The recipe for making soap is a simple one: lye + water + fat = soap. The process of making soap wasn't quite so simple; it took most of a day to make one barrel of soap and was done outdoors because of the strong smells and mess involved. Colonists usually only made soap once or twice a year.

To make soap, the colonists first prepared tallow. They hung a large kettle over an outdoor fire and filled it with cooking grease and animal fat they had saved. It took about 20 to 25 pounds of fat and grease to make one barrel of soap.

The fat and grease then had to be rendered to produce tallow. Tallow was used in both soap and candlemaking. This process involved cooking the fat and grease with water and then skimming off the grease that floated to the top. The grease was strained to remove impurities. This sometimes had to be done two or three times before the tallow could be used.

To obtain lye, they poured hot water through a tub called a leach barrel filled with ashes. The water filtered through the ashes out a hole in the barrel, forming lye. It took five or six large buckets of ashes to produce enough lye for one barrel of soap.

Working with lye is dangerous because it can cause terrible burns to the skin or eyes. Fumes can burn the lungs. If swallowed, it is poisonous.

Lye and tallow were then mixed together in the kettle with water and boiled until they formed a jelly-like substance. This substance, called soft soap, was stored in a barrel and used as needed.

1. If people still had to carry all the water for every bath into the house in buckets, heat it on the stove, dump it into the bathtub, and take a bath in an unheated room, how often do you think they would bathe?

    _____

2. What ingredients were used to make soap? _____

    _____

    _____

    _____

3. Why was soapmaking done outdoors? _____

    _____

    _____

4. Why was soapmaking dangerous? _____

    _____

    _____

Name: _____ Date: _____

Dyeing for Color

Not only did most of the colonists have to spin thread, weave their own fabrics, and sew their own clothes, they also had to dye the fabrics if they wanted colors. By using plants that grew in their gardens or in the woods, they were able to produce many different colors.

- For brown, colonists used a strong tea solution.
- The dry skins of yellow onions make a yellow dye.
- Strawberries or raspberries produce pink.
- Blueberries and purple grapes make a blue or purple dye.
- Spinach produces green dye.
- The pulp of grated beets can be used for red.

1. What other plants might be used to make dye? _____

_____

Work as a group. Each member should dye three strips of fabric in three different colors. This can be a messy project. Be sure to protect your work area with newspapers, a tarp, or an old plastic tablecloth. Wear old clothes or an apron.

A. Cut strips of white fabric about 2 inches wide and 2 feet long. Only natural fabrics like cotton or wool will work. An old white T-shirt can be used if it is 100% cotton.
B. Make your dyes in large plastic bowls. Pour hot water over the plants you use. Let the bowls sit overnight.
C. Remove the plant products before adding fabric.
D. Wet the fabric thoroughly before dyeing.
E. Stir the fabric in the dye so the color is even. The longer the fabric stays in the dye, the darker it will be.
F. Wring out the fabric completely when finished, then rinse it in cold water to set the color.
G. Hang the fabric to dry.

2. What colors did you produce? _____

_____

3. What did you use to make your colors? _____

_____

_____

When your three strips of fabric are dry, sew or tie them together at one end, then braid them. Coil the braid and stitch the coils together to make a mini mat.

Name: _____ Date: _____

Colonial Quilts

Colonial women made quilts by hand-sewing pieces of fabric together to form a design. The fabric was cut from different pieces of old or outgrown clothing. They attached a backing and stuffed the middle with a soft material such as cotton, goose down, or wool. To keep the stuffing in place, they sewed through all three layers, usually in a decorative pattern.

Because sewing materials were scarce and women had few outlets for artistic expression, quilts became a way to create something beautiful as well as practical. Quiltmakers displayed their work at fairs, and prizes were given for original designs. Quilts were often given as gifts for weddings or other special occasions.

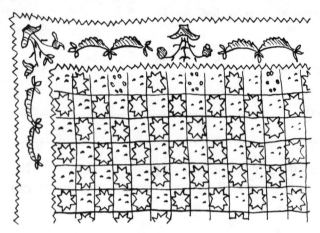

Besides being beautiful, quilts had a very practical purpose: they helped keep people warm on cold winter nights.

Making a large quilt took many hours. Sometimes several women got together for a "quilting bee." They all made individual squares and then sewed the squares together to make the finished quilt.

Quilting bees helped women finish their quilts more quickly and gave them an opportunity to sit with their friends and visit while they worked.

1. Many of the quilts made were called "patchwork" quilts. Why do you think this term was used?

    _____

    _____

2. Check out some quilt patterns by looking though quilting books from the library or patterns on the Internet. List one reference book or website you found.

    _____

3. Hold a quilting bee. Each person in the group can make one or more paper quilt squares. You can use one of the designs you found or make up your own.

    A. For each quilt square, cut a piece of graph paper into an eight- or nine-inch square. (Make sure everyone in the group makes the same size square.)

    B. Cut and glue paper to complete your design on the graph paper. Suggestions: wallpaper scraps, color ads from magazines, wrapping paper, etc.

    C. When finished, join quilt squares together with cellophane tape on the back side. Display the finished quilt for everyone to enjoy.

Name: _____ Date: _____

From Wool to Clothing

In spring, colonists sheared sheep. The heavy winter wool they cut from the animals could be turned into clothing for the colonists—with a bit of work.

When first cut, wool is oily, dirty, and matted. Sticks, leaves, and burrs had to be removed from the tangled fleece. The wool was then washed and carded. Carding means to fluff and straighten the fibers.

Spinning is the process of making yarn or thread from a fiber, such as wool, cotton, flax, or jute. Colonists used a spinning wheel and a distaff—a stick that held a bundle of the fiber for spinning. A foot pedal turned the wheel joining the fibers into a continuous length for use in weaving or knitting. Wool was dyed either before or after spinning.

The next step was to weave the yarn on a loom to make cloth. The cloth could then be cut and sewn to make clothing.

1. Why do you think sheep are sheared in spring, not fall?

   _____

   _____

2. Describe what you think it would be like to hold a large, uncooperative sheep still while someone cut off its wool.

   _____

   _____

3. Which job would you have rather done, shearing sheep or cleaning wool? Why?

   _____

   _____

4. Colonists wore "homespun" clothing. What do you think homespun means?

   _____

   _____

5. Number the steps for making wool into clothing in order.

   _____ spin wool into yarn
   _____ shear sheep
   _____ dye, cut, and sew clothes
   _____ clean wool
   _____ weave yarn into cloth

Did You Know? Cloth woven from flax is called linen.

Name: _____ Date: _____

Weaving

When the colonists arrived, many brought their looms. Some looms were so large, they took up almost an entire room. Many women learned basic weaving, while skilled artisans wove complex, beautiful designs.

Weaving is the process of interlacing pliable materials, usually at right angles to each other. Cloth is woven from yarn. Weaving can be quite simple or very complex, depending on the materials used and the size, shape, and pattern desired. Baskets can be woven from various plant materials such as reeds or vines. Other materials can be used for weaving mats and rugs.

1. To understand weaving, create a simple design with strips of colored construction paper. For more complicated designs, you can use more than two colors or paper strips in varying widths.

   Materials for simple paper weaving:
   Ten 12" x 1" strips of dark-colored construction paper
   Twenty 12" x $\frac{1}{2}$" strips of light-colored construction paper
   One 10" x 10" piece of cardboard
   Cellophane or masking tape

   A. Place the dark-colored strips side-by-side across the cardboard. Do not allow the strips to overlap. Turn over the one inch overhang on both ends. Tape ends securely to the back of the cardboard.

   B. Turn the cardboard 90°.

   C. Begin the first row by weaving a light-colored strip over the first dark strip, under the second, over, under, etc.

   D. Tape the one-inch overhang on both ends of the light-colored strip to the back of the cardboard.

   E. Begin the second row by weaving another light-colored strip next to the first one. This time go under the first dark strip, over the second, under, over, etc. Tape ends as before.

   F. Repeat steps C to E until all light-colored strips are used.

2. What other materials could you use for weaving projects? _____

   _____

3. Many weaving project ideas can be found in books, at craft stores, and on the Internet. Check out those sources to learn more about weaving.

Name: _____ Date: _____

Make a Sampler

Girls as young as five or six were taught to make samplers. Making a sampler served more than one purpose. Since many girls did not have an opportunity to go to school, they learned the alphabet while they learned to sew.

A young girl's first sampler project might be to embroider a long piece of linen with the letters of the alphabet drawn on by an adult. Older girls embroidered samplers with the multiplication tables, pictures, or words to Bible verses.

As they gained experience, women's samplers might contain elaborate pictures of flowers and animals. Finished samplers were used as wall hangings or pillow covers.

Combining several different stitches and colors of thread adds texture and makes samplers more interesting. Three common stitches are shown.

chain stitch

cross-stitch

stem or outline stitch

Try making your own sampler.

1. Practice making the three types of stitches shown. Use a white or light-colored washcloth for material.

2. Thread a darning needle with yarn and make a knot at the end. Practice one type of stitch at a time. When you finish, tie off the yarn on the back of the washcloth.

3. After you've practiced each type of stitch, cut and remove the practice stitches.

4. Make a simple sampler by neatly printing your name with chalk in large block letters. Use any of the stitches you practiced or a combination of them to embroider your name. You can add flowers, animals, or other designs to your sampler to make it more elaborate.

5. If you like your sampler, you can frame it and hang it for a decoration. If you don't, remove the stitches and return the washcloth to the drawer.

Name: _____ Date: _____

Spice Up Your Life

The smells in colonial homes must have been rather strong at times. Some of the smells, like bread baking, would have been pleasant. Other smells might not have been so pleasant.

1. Imagine walking into a one-room log cabin where a family cooks, eats, sleeps, and occasionally bathes. Herbs, spices, fruit, and meat hang from the rafters. The fireplace is burning. Someone is smoking a corncob pipe. Close your eyes and take a deep breath. Describe what you smell.

   _____

   _____

   _____

To overcome some of the more unpleasant odors, colonial women used dried flower petals for sachets and made pomander balls.

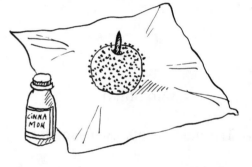

Follow these steps to make a pomander ball.

A. Select a firm, ripe apple, orange, lemon, or lime.

B. Use a toothpick or small nail to prick small holes in the fruit skin. Gently push a whole clove into each hole until the entire surface of the fruit is covered.

C. Bend a wire paperclip into a u-shape. Push the tips of the paperclip into the stem of the fruit for a handle. Roll the fruit in ground cinnamon or allspice.

D. Cut a square of cheesecloth large enough to wrap around the fruit. Place the fruit in the center of the cheesecloth. Gather the corners of the cheesecloth together around the paperclip. Tightly tie it closed with string or a pretty ribbon.

   Describe the smell of your pomander ball: _____

   _____

E. Let the fruit dry in a cool, dark place, like a closet, for two to three weeks. Prick small holes in the cheesecloth. Hang the pomander ball where others can enjoy the delicious aroma.

   Describe the smell of your pomander ball now. _____

   _____

Did You Know? When colonists visited someone sick, they often carried pomander balls. They believed that if they smelled the pomander balls while visiting, they wouldn't catch the sickness.

Name: _____ Date: _____

Making Watertight Containers

Some of the dishes, cups, and other containers used by colonists were made of clay. Making clay dishes may not be as easy as you think.

<u>Here's your challenge:</u> Try to make a clay container that will hold water without leaking.

A.   Mold modeling clay into the desired shape.

B.   Decorate it any way you wish, but don't color it yet.

C.   Set your container in the sun to dry. You will probably need to wait several days before it is completely hard.

D.   Paint your container.

E.   Check to see if your container will hold water without leaking.

1. Did it work? _____

2. If not, what do you think you could have done differently?

    _____

    _____

    _____

3. If it did hold water, how do you think you could have made your container better?

    _____

    _____

    _____

4. After your container dried, did the shape remain the same?

    _____

5. If not, why do you think it changed?

    _____

    _____

    _____

6. If your container turned out, use it to display flowers or as a pencil holder. **CAUTION: Do not drink or eat from any homemade clay container.**

27

Name: _____ Date: _____

Tidbits of Colonial Trivia

- The town crier was a distinguished position in England and the colonies in the seventeenth and eighteenth centuries. Before printed materials were widely available, the town crier acted as a "walking newspaper," making his appointed rounds to the city's main street corners announcing town meetings, the time of day, and other news of interest.

- In 1654, it cost two shillings for horses, cows, and oxen and one shilling for hogs, sheep, and goats to cross a toll bridge over the Newbury River in Massachusetts. People could cross for free.

- In 1656, Captain Kemble of Boston was sentenced to sit in the stocks for two hours because of his unseemly behavior in public on a Sunday. He had kissed his wife after returning from a three-year sea voyage!

- In 1660, Massachusetts passed a law forbidding any celebration of Christmas. Offenders were fined five shillings.

- The first coffee house in Boston was started in 1670 by a woman permitted to sell coffee and chocolate.

- In the Plymouth colony, this law was passed in 1674: "whosoever person ran a race with any horse in any street or common road should forfeit five shillings or sit in the stocks for one hour."

- Thirty men were arrested in Connecticut in 1674 for wearing silk and having long hair.

- In 1712, people who drove their wagons recklessly in Philadelphia were fined for speeding.

- The Liberty Bell was cast in England and delivered to Philadelphia in 1752. While being tested in Philadelphia, it cracked and had to be melted down and recast.

- The Rhode Island Assembly prohibited theatrical productions in 1761 and fined actors who broke the law.

- Public transportation was slow in the colonies. It took Thomas Jefferson five days to travel from Philadelphia to Baltimore in 1783.

1. Use reference sources to find two other interesting tidbits of colonial trivia.

_____

_____

_____

Name: _____ Date: _____

Make a Whirligig

One of the homemade toys children in the colonies played with was a whirligig. In colonial times, a whirligig might have been made by cutting a thin slice of wood from a three- to four-inch diameter tree branch and using a nail to punch the center holes.

Make a Whirligig:

1. Use the pattern below to cut a circle from heavy cardboard.

2. Punch holes in the center as shown on the pattern.

3. Use markers to create a colorful geometric design on both sides of the circle. (Spirals or concentric circles look great.)

4. Thread about $2\frac{1}{2}$ feet of string through the holes, and tie the ends together.

5. Hold the string between the thumb and index finger of both hands. Twirl until the string is tight.

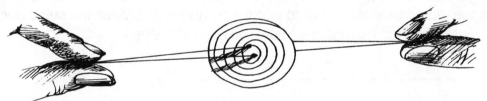

6. Stretch out the string to make the whirligig spin. By pulling and relaxing the tension on the string, you can keep it going for quite a while. Hold contests to see who can keep the whirligig spinning the longest.

7. Listen as the whirligig spins. Why do you think it's called a whirligig?

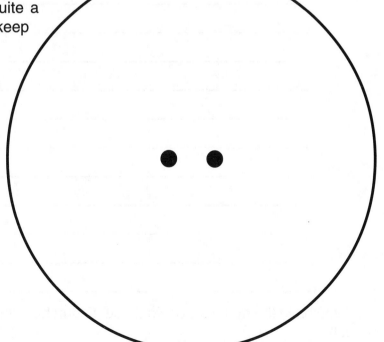

   _____

   _____

   _____

   _____

   _____

   _____

   _____

Name: _____ Date: _____

Cornhusk Dolls

Colonial children had little time to play and few toys to play with in the New World. The toys they did have were handmade and usually quite simple.

Native Americans made cornhusk dolls for their children long before the colonists arrived. They fashioned the dried husks (outer covering of corn on the cob) into a figure resembling a person. Making a cornhusk doll was one of many things the colonists learned in the New World.

1. Why didn't anyone in Europe make cornhusk dolls before they came to America?

    _____

    _____

2. Making a cornhusk doll is a craft people still enjoy today. Use the Internet, library, or other reference materials to learn how to make a cornhusk doll. Write the steps needed to make a cornhusk doll. Add illustrations to demonstrate the steps.

    _____

    _____

    _____

    _____

    _____

    _____

    _____

    _____

    _____

    _____

    _____

    _____

If you have the materials or would like to purchase them at a craft store, try making a cornhusk doll.

Name: _____ Date: _____

Nine Men's Morris

Nine Men's Morris (also called Mill) was a game played in colonial times. The game board could be drawn on paper, painted on wood, or even drawn in the dirt with a stick. Playing pieces were whatever was handy, like small stones, wood chips, peas, beans, or kernels of corn.

Read the rules for this game, make a game board, find something to use for game pieces, and play it with a partner.

Rules:

A.   Each player has nine game pieces. Players take turns putting one game piece on the board at any point where lines meet.

B.   The object is to get three of your game pieces in a row and to prevent the other player from doing the same.

C.   When a player gets three game pieces in a row, he or she takes one of the opponent's playing pieces off the board.

D.   After all playing pieces are placed, a game piece can be moved by sliding it to any connecting space that is empty.

E.   Game ends when one player is left with only two game pieces.

This is how the game board looks:

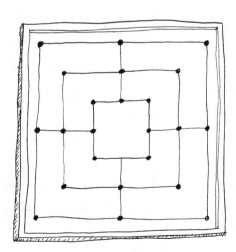

1.   What did you use for game pieces?_____

2.   Did you like the game? _____ Why or why not? _____

_____

Name: _____ Date: _____

Many Skills Needed

Colonists needed many skills to survive in the New World. They needed to hunt, trap, fish, chop down trees, build homes, plant crops, spin wool, make cloth, sew, bake bread, churn butter, make soap and candles, milk cows, and raise farm animals.

Some colonists specialized in skills like medicine, law, blacksmithing, barrelmaking, or wigmaking. They sold or traded their services or the goods they made for what they needed.

1. Work with a group. Brainstorm to add more occupations to the list below. Use another piece of paper to continue your list. Include jobs that are done today as well as ones that were done in colonial times. For each job, put a check in the appropriate column. For some jobs, both columns could be checked.

	Today	Colonial
news announcer	_____	_____
teacher	_____	_____
journalist	_____	_____
blacksmith	_____	_____
barber	_____	_____
astronaut	_____	_____
_____	_____	_____
_____	_____	_____
_____	_____	_____
_____	_____	_____
_____	_____	_____
_____	_____	_____
_____	_____	_____
_____	_____	_____
_____	_____	_____
_____	_____	_____

2. When finished, fill in this chart.

Total jobs listed _____

Jobs done only today _____

Jobs done only in colonial times _____

Jobs done both then and now _____

Name: _____ Date: _____

Livestock

The animals colonists raised needed to be fed, watered, sheltered from the cold, and protected from wild animals. Although this meant additional work for the colonists, livestock also provided many necessities.

1. Colonists raised oxen and horses to help them work. What types of work could oxen and horses do?

_____

_____

_____

2. Horses were important for transportation. Why?

_____

_____

_____

3. Colonists raised pigs, cows, sheep, geese, and chickens for food. What types of food did these animals provide?

_____

_____

_____

4. Besides food, what else did these animals provide? Be specific.

_____

_____

_____

5. Dogs were often part of the colonial farmstead, but not merely as pets. Dogs also helped farmers in several ways. List ways dogs would have been useful to colonists.

_____

_____

_____

6. Which two animals do you think were most important to colonists? Why?

_____

_____

_____

Name: _____ Date: _____

Trading for Goods and Services

Rather than paying for goods and services with money, colonists often used the barter system. A woman who raised chickens might trade eggs for milk or butter with a neighbor who had a cow. A blacksmith might make horseshoes in exchange for several loaves of homemade bread and some jam. The items exchanged would be approximately equal in value.

What do you think would have been a fair trade for each of these items?

Product or Service   **Something of Equivalent Value**

1. handmade quilt   _____

2. dozen eggs   _____

3. bushel of apples   _____

4. bushel of potatoes   _____

5. doctor visit for a sick child   _____

6. basket of fresh berries   _____

7. pound of fresh honey   _____

8. pound of fresh butter   _____

9. ten pounds of flour   _____

10. ten bars of homemade soap   _____

11. 25 homemade candles   _____

12. four new wagon wheels   _____

13. four horseshoes   _____

14. large pile of fireplace wood   _____

15. large iron soup kettle   _____

16. new wooden barrel   _____

17. 100 iron nails   _____

18. ten jars of fresh jam   _____

19. bushel of corn   _____

20. five yards of woven wool cloth   _____

Name: _____ Date: _____

The Importance of Water

Having a nearby source of fresh water was critical to the colonists. It was needed for cooking, drinking, watering crops, feeding livestock, bathing, and putting out fires. Without a source of water, colonists wouldn't have had a source of power to run gristmills. Metalworkers needed water to cool items they made. Papermakers needed water to make paper. Water was also a major means of transportation.

1. List eight ways people today use water for personal needs at home and at school.

   _____

   _____

   _____

   _____

   _____

   _____

   _____

   _____

2. List eight other ways people in your community use water.

   _____

   _____

   _____

   _____

   _____

   _____

   _____

   _____

3. Do you think water is more or less important to a community today than it was in colonial times? Explain your answer.

   _____

   _____

   _____

   _____

Name: _____ Date: _____

Millers

   Millers were important members of a colonial community. To make bread, people needed flour. Wheat, corn, rye, and oats are tough grains that must be ground to produce flour or meal.

   Grinding grain by hand is a very difficult job. When enough settlers lived in an area, they built a gristmill. Farmers would travel many miles to have their grain made into flour or meal.

   The gristmill needed power to move the machinery used to grind grain. Without electricity, the power needed was usually provided by moving water. Gristmills were built beside streams or rivers. A dam built across the stream created a millpond. The millpond provided a steady flow of water to the waterwheel, which used gears to turn a millstone and grind the grain.

1. Use reference sources to find out more about how a gristmill worked. Draw a diagram to show how a waterwheel, gears, and millstone were used to grind grain.

2. Look in your local telephone book. How many entries for the name Miller are there?

_____

Did You Know? Like the general store, the gristmill was a community gathering place for people to meet and exchange news.

Name: _____ Date: _____

The Importance of Sawmills

If colonists wanted wooden planks before sawmills were built, they had to chop down trees and cut the logs into boards. They used a broadax to square logs or a two-person whipsaw to make planks. Producing one plank required much time and energy, and they needed hundreds of boards to build one house.

Without a sawmill, building a house, barn, or other structure was a major undertaking. That's why many of the early buildings were made of logs.

Sawmills, like gristmills, depended on water power. Water power could also be used to transport logs from where they were cut downstream to the sawmill.

Once a sawmill was built in a settlement, the village tended to grow more quickly. People moved to areas with sawmills because they could build houses and shops more easily. More people and available lumber encouraged woodworkers like carpenters, cabinetmakers, coopers, wheelwrights, and wainwrights to set up shops nearby.

1. Use reference sources. Write a paragraph explaining how logs were made into planks at a sawmill.

_____

_____

_____

_____

_____

_____

_____

_____

_____

_____

Did You Know? People who sawed planks from logs were called sawyers. Do you know anyone whose last name is Sawyer?

    37

Name: _____ Date: _____

Coopers

Do you know anyone whose last name is Cooper? Chances are, one of that person's ancestors was a real cooper—a person who made wooden barrels, buckets, pails, tubs, and piggins. Colonists used these containers to store everything from nails to pickles to eggs. A good barrel had to be watertight and could be used to store liquids.

A cooper made a barrel by binding wooden planks, called staves, together with wooden or metal hoops. Staves were carved from large pieces of oak, pine, or cedar and shaped so they were wider in the middle and narrower at the ends.

The cooper used a trussing ring to hold the staves upright in a circle, while he pulled them tightly together using a rope, crank, and windlass.

Then the cooper placed hoops around the staves to keep everything in place. The tops and bottoms of barrels were cut from wide planks of wood. A hole in the top of the barrel allowed liquids to be poured in or out of the barrel. A tightfitting wooden peg was used to close the hole to prevent spilling or evaporation.

1. Use reference sources. What is a piggin? Draw a picture to show what it looked like.

    _____

    _____

    _____

    _____

2. Why do you think coopers made staves in the shape they did?

    _____

    _____

    _____

    _____

3. Use a dictionary to define *windlass.*

    _____

    _____

Did You Know? Ships sailing between England and the New World were required by law to have at least one master cooper as part of the crew. His job was to oversee barrels containing water and other provisions and to prevent any of the barrels from leaking.

Name: _____ Date: _____

Cabinetmakers

"All the countrey is overgrowne with trees ..." wrote Captain John Smith when he came to Jamestown in 1607. Trees were one of the most valuable resources the colonists found in the New World.

In colonial times, all furniture was made by hand. Most people learned to make some of their own furniture, like tables, chairs, benches, and bed frames. The furniture they made was strong, heavy, and practical but, for the most part, not very beautiful. Many people did not have the skills, time, or tools to make fine furniture. That work was done by cabinetmakers.

Cabinetmakers created many elegant pieces of furniture held together without glue or nails. This was done by hand carving precise joints that fit together perfectly. Sometimes cabinetmakers were called joiners, because they were experts at connecting pieces of wood in ways that were strong, neat, and almost invisible.

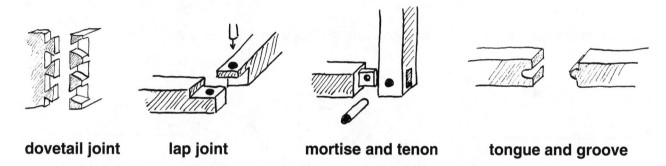

dovetail joint   **lap joint**   **mortise and tenon**   **tongue and groove**

Cabinetmakers used many hand tools in their work including saws, hammers, drills, mallets, planes, chisels, knives, and lathes.

To give furniture a beautiful finish, the cabinetmaker used stain, vegetable dye, oil, or varnish. Polishing and rubbing in the finish was a job often done by the cabinetmaker's apprentice.

Besides making fine furniture, cabinetmakers also made and repaired musical instruments, repaired furniture, and even made coffins.

Use reference sources.

1. What is a lathe? _____

   _____

   _____

2. What does a woodworker use a lathe for? _____

   _____

   _____

Did You Know? Since the cabinetmaker made coffins, he often took care of funeral arrangements as well.

Name: _____ Date: _____

Wheelwrights

Colonists needed wagons and carts for transportation and to haul goods. Since wheels were made of wood and roads were rough and bumpy, wheels needed frequent repair. Wheelwrights made and repaired wooden wheels.

To make a wooden wheel, the wheelwright started with the hub. This was the center of a wheel and needed to be the strongest part. It was made from very hard wood, aged for several years. Spokes were attached to the hub to give the rim strength. The axle, made of cast iron, ran through the center of the hub. The rim of the wheel was made of curved sections of wood called felloes, joined to make a full circle.

To finish a wheel, an iron ring, slightly smaller than the rim, was heated so it would expand enough to fit tightly around the rim. The wheelwright then hammered the iron ring onto the rim while it was still hot. When it cooled, the iron ring contracted and fit tightly around the rim.

1. Label the hub, spokes, rim, and iron ring on this wheel.

A. _____

B. _____

C. _____

D. _____

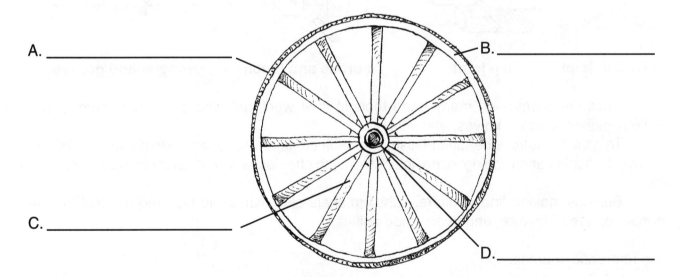

2. Wheelwrights made wheels, but we don't usually say that wainwrights made wains. What did wainwrights make?

_____

3. What did wheelwrights, wainwrights, cabinetmakers, and coopers have in common?

_____

_____

_____

_____

Name: _____ Date: _____

Blacksmiths

When people picture a blacksmith from the colonial period, they often think of a person making horseshoes. Making shoes for horses and oxen was part of a blacksmith's job but a minor one. The blacksmith created fireplace and kitchen utensils, kettles, guns, pots and pans, metal hoops for barrels, and farm tools. He also made latches, locks, and nails.

The blacksmith worked at a raised brick hearth called a forge. A coal fire provided the heat needed to make iron soft enough to bend. He used a large bellows to fan the flames and keep the fire hot.

Blacksmiths used other tools in their work including tongs to hold the hot metal, hammers to pound metal into the desired shape, and an anvil, which was a large, cast-iron block. The blacksmith hammered his pieces into shape on the anvil.

To change the shape of iron, the blacksmith heated it until it became malleable and then hammered it on the anvil.

During the Revolutionary War, blacksmiths were kept very busy making cannons, cannon balls, and other tools of war. The Continental Congress hired Peter Townsend, a blacksmith, to make a huge iron chain long enough to stretch across the narrow part of the Hudson River near West Point to stop British warships. Each link of the chain was about one foot by three feet. In all, it measured about 500 yards. Held in place by iron anchors, which Townsend also made, the chain did its job. No British warships were able to sail past it.

1. Use reference sources. Draw a picture of an anvil.

2. Use a dictionary. What does *malleable* mean? _____

3. A farrier was a specialized type of blacksmith. What did a farrier do? _____
   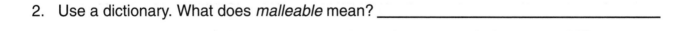

Did You Know? The word *smith* comes from *smite* (to hit or pound something). A blacksmith worked mostly with iron, which is black. So the word *blacksmith* means "a person who pounds black metal."

Name: _____ Date: _____

Pewterers and Silversmiths

Once colonists had most of the necessities they needed for daily life, they also wanted items that were decorative and beautiful.

People who worked as pewterers and silversmiths were artisans. They poured hot, melted metal into molds formed in the shape of the item they wished to produce: shoe buckles, buttons, candleholders, dishes, spoons, cups, and teapots. Silversmiths worked with gold, brass, and copper as well as silver.

Paul Revere was one of the best known silversmiths during the colonial period. He was born in Boston in 1735. The son of a silversmith, he became a silversmith and engraver. He was well known during his lifetime as a designer of elegant silverware, tankards, bowls, plates, pitchers, and tea sets. He also designed the first seal for the united colonies as well as the seal still used by Massachusetts.

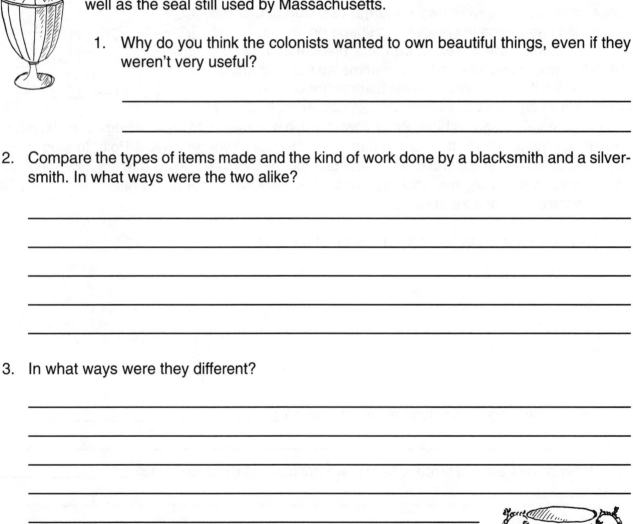

1. Why do you think the colonists wanted to own beautiful things, even if they weren't very useful?

    _____

    _____

2. Compare the types of items made and the kind of work done by a blacksmith and a silversmith. In what ways were the two alike?

    _____

    _____

    _____

    _____

    _____

3. In what ways were they different?

    _____

    _____

    _____

    _____

Did You Know? Paul Revere also made artificial teeth, surgical instruments, engraved printing plates, and printed money for the Massachusetts Congress.

Name: _____ Date: _____

Tinsmiths

Tin is a soft, silvery metal used to make pails, lanterns, and kitchen utensils. A tinsmith hammered sheets of tin into useful shapes. He also made and repaired lightweight pots and pans. Records show that Paul Revere, a silversmith, also made tinware.

Decorative tinware was one of the arts practiced in colonial times. Designs were punched or pierced into a piece of tin in decorative patterns.

Tinsmiths cut the tin to shape and then embossed a pattern on it by gently striking a punch with a hammer to form depressions in the tin.

To make tin-punch art, you will need a square of heavy cardboard, a piece of aluminum foil larger than the cardboard, tape, a two- to three-inch finishing nail (one with a small, rounded top), graph paper, and a pencil.

1. Cover the cardboard with the aluminum foil, wrapping the excess around the back.

2. Smooth the aluminum foil, and use tape on the back to hold it firmly in place.

3. Draw a design on graph paper the same size as your cardboard. Use the top of the nail to impress the design on the aluminum-covered cardboard. Press firmly to indent the design but not too hard that you rip the foil.

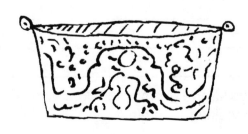

43

Name: _____ Date: _____

Leatherworkers

In the colonies, people depended on horses for work and transportation. They needed saddles and harnesses for their horses, mules, and oxen. These items were made by harnessmakers.

A harnessmaker used leather from the hides of cows and buffalo. He prepared the hides by tanning them or bought hides already tanned. Tanning is a process of curing and preserving hides to make the leather soft and flexible. The harnessmaker carefully cut pieces of leather and stitched them together.

The shoemaker made leather shoes and boots for men and women. Before starting to make shoes, however, a shoemaker needed to carve a last. Lasts are blocks of wood carved into foot shapes. A shoemaker needed many different sizes of lasts to be able to make shoes for children, women, and men. Lasts could be used over and over.

First, the shoemaker stretched the leather upper of the shoe over the last. Then he cut the sole and pounded it into shape with a hammer. Using an awl, the shoemaker made holes in the thick leather. He used waxed thread to sew the sole and upper parts of the shoes together. A good shoemaker could finish two pairs of shoes in one 12-hour workday.

When a shoemaker made a pair of shoes or boots, both the left and right were the same size and shape. People didn't have many choices for sizes of the shoes and boots they bought. Shoes came in small, medium, and large. People with very small, large, narrow, or wide feet would need to pay extra, so the shoemaker could make a special last for that person's specific size.

1. Use a dictionary. What is a harness?

    _____

    _____

2. Draw a picture of an awl. Use a reference book if you don't know what an awl looks like.

3. What advantage was there to the shoemaker in not having to make different shaped shoes for the right and left feet?

    _____

    _____

    _____

Did You Know? The London shoemakers' guild, the Worshipful Company of Cordwainers, helped finance Captain John Smith's 1607 expedition to Virginia.

Name: _____ Date: _____

Papermakers

At first, every piece of paper used by the colonists had to be imported from Europe. As the colonies grew, the demand for paper increased. People used paper for writing letters. Merchants wanted paper to record sales. People needed paper for keeping official records, and printers needed paper for books, pamphlets, and newspapers.

In colonial days, paper was made from cotton or linen rags. However, the colonists had few rags to spare for papermaking. They had too many other uses for cloth. Most paper in the colonies was imported, and it was expensive.

To make paper, rags were cut up, washed, and boiled until the cloth broke into tiny pieces called pulp. The papermaker strained the pulp through a sieve and formed it into sheets of paper. The newly-made sheets of paper were pressed to remove the water and then hung on racks to dry.

To complete the process, papermakers made gelatine by boiling the hooves, bones, and hides of animals. Paper was then dipped in a mixture of gelatine and water, pressed, and allowed to dry.

The British were not happy when the colonists began printing articles that called for freedom from England. When the Revolutionary War began, England stopped exporting paper to the colonies. This caused such a paper shortage that anyone who was skilled at papermaking was excused from the army to work making paper.

1. List three things besides paper colonists may have used to write on and tools they might have used to write with.

   Example: slate and chalk.

   _____

   _____

   _____

   _____

2. People also wrote on parchment. Use a reference source. What is parchment?

   _____

   _____

   _____

   _____

Did You Know? In 1688, William Rittenhouse, a master papermaker, arrived in German-Town near Philadelphia. He helped build the first papermill in America.

Name: _____ Date: _____

Printers

Printing is a method of pressing letters, words, sentences, and pictures onto sheets of paper. Whether they printed their own words or the words of others, printers influenced the thoughts and opinions of their fellow colonists.

The Reverend Jose Glover, the first printer to sail for the New World, never arrived. He and Stephen Daye, a blacksmith hired to accompany him, loaded up the printing equipment and supplies and sailed from England with their families. However, Glover died at sea.

The families settled in Cambridge, and Mrs. Glover hired Stephen Daye to open a print shop. At that time, the political and religious leaders of the colony controlled everything that was printed. If they didn't approve, the printer could be arrested, fined, and put out of business.

The first item Daye printed in 1639 was "The Free-Man's Oath," a statement of allegiance that all colonists were required to sign. In 1640, Daye printed *The Whole Booke of Psalmes,* the first full-length book published in the New World.

Other printers set up shops in the colonies, but problems quickly arose because printers wanted to print whatever they wished.

Publick Occurrences, the first newspaper printed in Boston in 1690, was shut down after one issue because it criticized the British in their war with the French.

John Peter Zenger, editor of the *New-York Weekly Journal,* was arrested in 1735 for printing articles criticizing the government. His lawyer argued that although he had broken the law, the fact that he had printed the truth was more important. The jury did not convict Zenger. From this case came the idea of "freedom of the press."

1. What does "freedom of the press" mean to you?

_____

_____

_____

_____

_____

_____

2. Do you think newspapers should always have the right to print anything they want if it's true? Why or why not?

_____

_____

_____

_____

_____

_____

_____

Name: _____ Date: _____

Apprentices

In colonial times, there were no factories to produce goods. If a person needed a saddle, barrel, candlestick, wheel, or nail, someone had to make it. Specialists, called masters, in many trades produced these items.

People did not learn their jobs by attending schools. Sometimes children learned skills from their parents. Another way was for children between the ages of seven and 15 to become apprentices. Since women rarely worked outside their homes, most apprentices were boys.

A formal apprenticeship usually lasted between four and seven years. During that time, the master provided room, board, clothing, and training. In exchange for their training, apprentices worked hard without pay. They ran errands, did chores around the house or shop, and helped the master at his trade.

At the end of the apprenticeship, each person was required to produce a finished object called a masterpiece. If the object was good enough, the apprentice became a journeyman. The term journeyman came about because after completing their apprenticeships, many young men journeyed around the country, making and repairing goods until they saved enough money to open their own shops.

This system was very practical at the time and worked well if the master craftsman was a good person and skilled in his trade. Problems arose if the master was cruel and lazy.

1. Imagine being an apprentice in any skill or trade available today. Which type of job would you most like to learn? Why?

   _____

   _____

   _____

2. Compare today's education system to the apprentice system by listing three advantages to the apprentice system and three advantages to today's education system.

   a. Advantages of apprentice system: _____

   _____

   _____

   _____

   b. Advantages of today's system: _____

   _____

   _____

Name: _____ Date: _____

The Role of Colonial Women

Today women can choose careers in any occupation, but that was not true in colonial times. Few women worked outside their homes or ran their own businesses, although there were some exceptions. Some women became teachers, but even that was usually a man's job. The millinery shop, a place that made women's clothing, was one of the few businesses run by women.

Some women became artisans at various crafts, like candlemaking, quilting, or weaving, and were able to sell or trade the items they made. Most colonial women found homemaking and raising a family to be more than a full-time job.

Although they did not get paid for the work they did, women learned the skills needed for many occupations. Give examples of how the skills for these occupations were part of a woman's job in the home. The first one is completed for you.

1. baker: Women baked bread, cakes, and pies for their families.

2. barber: _____

3. butcher: _____

4. carpenter: _____

5. chemist: _____

6. cook: _____

7. doctor: _____

8. farmer: _____

9. gardener: _____

10. pharmacist: _____

11. seamstress: _____

12. teacher: _____

13. toymaker: _____

14. List six other occupations colonial women needed the skills and knowledge to perform.

_____

_____

_____

_____

Name: _____ Date: _____

Colonists Wanted

Wanted: Brave, healthy men, women, and children, willing to leave their homes, travel on crowded ships, relocate to an unknown land, face unknown dangers, and work long hours without pay. Only those seriously interested should apply.

The year is 1650. The king gave you permission to start a settlement in the New World. You will need people with useful skills for the new colony.

1. List the ten skills you think will be most important.

   _____   _____

   _____   _____

   _____   _____

   _____   _____

   _____   _____

2. Write a want ad of 25 words or less you could put in a newspaper to recruit people to join your colony. Be specific about the types of skills and experience people need to apply.

   _____

   _____

   _____

   _____

3. One thousand people answered your ad, but you can only take 100. Write ten questions you could ask the people who applied. Be sure to find out about their skills, hobbies, experience, training, and anything else you think is important to help you decide who would be best for your colony.

   1. _____
   2. _____
   3. _____
   4. _____
   5. _____
   6. _____
   7. _____
   8. _____
   9. _____
   10. _____

Name: _____ Date: _____

Life in a Colonial Village

Not everyone in the colonies lived on farms, nor did they all live in log cabins. As more colonists arrived, towns grew larger in places like Boston, Jamestown, and Williamsburg. Founded in 1630, Boston had a population of 7,000 and was the largest city in the colonies by 1700.

When ships arrived from Europe, the colonists searched for a pleasant place that had trees for lumber, land suitable for farming, and streams for fresh water. This is how they decided where to build their settlements.

Ships were the only way to travel to and from Europe. The farther from the coast people lived, the more difficult it was to transport supplies that arrived from Europe. Eventually, as the economy grew, people wanted to be near a port so they could ship their goods back to Europe in trade.

Since there were few roads, even a distance of ten miles would have been a long journey. A horse-drawn wagon could travel about two and one-half miles an hour in good weather. In winter or when it rained hard, traveling could be even slower.

As cities grew, houses tended to be larger and made of wooden planks, rather than logs. Those with specialized skills set up shops if there were enough people in the area to buy or trade for their goods and services.

1. Use an atlas. Find a city in your state with a population of about 7,000. _____

2. What's the population of your city? _____

3. If someone lived ten miles away, how long would it take to travel to the coast in a horse-drawn wagon?

   _____

4. How long would it have taken to make the round trip to the coast and back home?

   _____

5. Give three examples of **goods** that specialists in a colonial village may have provided.

   _____   _____   _____

6. Give three examples of **services** that specialists in a colonial village may have provided.

   _____   _____   _____

7. Use reference sources. Besides homes, what other buildings would have been found in a colonial city?

   _____

   _____

   _____

   _____

Name: _____ Date: _____

Community Spirit

Life for the early colonists must have been quite lonely at times. Many people lived in isolated areas. A colonist's community might consist of only the immediate family. The nearest neighbors may have been several miles away. As more people arrived in an area and set up homes, a community spirit began to develop.

The community spirit of the colonists could be seen in the ways neighbors helped each other. When big jobs needed to be done, such as building a barn or a house, neighbors joined together for a "barn raising" or a "house raising." Everyone worked together to cut the wood and build what was needed.

"Bees" were another popular way for people to cooperate to complete a large project. Quilting bees, sewing bees, and corn husking bees were social occasions as well as work sessions.

1. Use a dictionary to define *community.* _____

_____

2. What is "community spirit"? _____

_____

_____

3. If five families in a community all needed to build barns, what would be the advantage of working as a group to build all of them rather than having each individual family build its own?

_____

_____

4. If one of the five families didn't need a barn, why would it be in their best interest to help anyway?

_____

_____

5. If your neighbors asked you to rake their large lawn for $20, would you rather do it alone and earn all the money or share the job and the money with friends? Why?

_____

_____

6. How do people in your community help each other?

_____

_____

Name: _____ Date: _____

Shopping at the General Store

While colonists waited for their grain to be ground at the gristmill, they might stop at the town's general store. The general store was more than a place to buy items. It was also a gathering place for people to meet, visit, and exchange news.

The general store became the trading center in most colonial villages. Some goods in the store were imported from Europe. Others were items brought in by farmers, homemakers, hunters, trappers, and craftsmen.

The shopkeeper kept track of sales and trades. If a blacksmith brought a keg of nails to the general store, he could either trade them for things he needed or receive credit for later purchases. The shopkeeper made a small profit on each transaction.

A general store was part grocery store, part clothing store, part hardware store, part bookstore, part specialty shop, and part pharmacy. You might find hundreds of items for sale, including nails, guns, sugar, salt, shoes, soap, cloth, furs, rope, tools, pots, pails, paper, and medicine.

1. Brainstorm with a partner to fill in the chart from "A" to "Z" with items that might have been sold at the general store. (If you can't think of one for "X" or "Z," that's okay.)

A _____	N _____
B _____	O _____
C _____	P _____
D _____	Q _____
E _____	R _____
F _____	S _____
G _____	T _____
H _____	U _____
I _____	V _____
J _____	W _____
K _____	X _____
L _____	Y _____
M _____	Z _____

Did You Know? The general store often served as the community's post office.

Name: _____ Date: _____

Colonial Education

As colonial settlements grew, the people built schools for their children. Most schools contained only one room with wooden desks. One teacher taught all the children from first through eighth grades. Older students helped teach younger ones.

Teachers were paid by members of the community, sometimes in money, but more often in goods and services. Families took turns providing room and board for the teacher.

Children learned the "three R's" in school—reading, (w)riting, and (a)rithmetic.

Schools had very few books and maps, no libraries, and of course, no media center. At first, paper was too expensive to use except for very special letters and documents. Instead, children wrote on small pieces of slate with chalk or slate pencils. The advantage of this method was that the slates could be wiped clean and reused over and over.

1. Do you think you would have liked attending a one-room schoolhouse? Why or why not?

   _____

   _____

   _____

2. What term do we use today for arithmetic?

   _____

3. Besides the "three R's", what else do students learn in school today?

   _____

   _____

   _____

4. Use reference sources. What is slate?

   _____

   _____

5. List items found in your classroom that probably weren't available to colonial children.

   _____

   _____

   _____

Name: _____ Date: _____

Make a Quill Pen

The colonists used quill pens and ink to write their letters and important documents. Quill pens were made from the wing feathers of geese, turkeys, and other large birds. Thomas Jefferson wrote the Declaration of Independence using a quill pen.

Make your own quill pen and ink by following these steps.

1. Soak a large feather (about 10 inches long) in warm soapy water for 15 minutes. Dry it with a paper towel.

2. Cut off the bottom two inches of the tip with scissors. Cut at an angle. This is the point of the pen called the nib.

3. Use a pin or toothpick to carefully clean out the center of the nib.

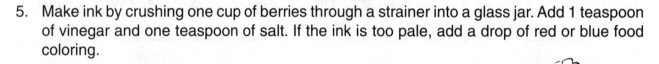

4. Cut a small slit in the nib. This helps control the flow of ink.

5. Make ink by crushing one cup of berries through a strainer into a glass jar. Add 1 teaspoon of vinegar and one teaspoon of salt. If the ink is too pale, add a drop of red or blue food coloring.

    CAUTION: Cover your work area with newspapers. Do not spill ink on your clothes. It may leave a permanent stain.

6. To write, tip the nib into the ink. Press off the excess ink on a paper towel. Hold the quill at an angle, and write with the tip. Repeat this step when your pen runs out of ink.

7. Use your quill pen and ink to sign your name in large letters like John Hancock did on the Declaration of Independence.

Besides crushed berries, what other items could you use to make your own ink?

_____

_____

_____

_____

_____

_____

Name: _____ Date: _____

Rules of Civility & Decent Behaviour in Company and Conversation

Children in the colonies learned to read and write by copying from other sources —over and over. As they wrote, they were expected to learn. When George Washington was a boy, there were over 100 "Rules of Civility & Decent Behaviour In Company and Conversation" to be written and learned. Notice that the spelling, capitalization, and punctuation used was much different.

Rewrite each rule using modern words and grammar on another sheet of paper. Use a dictionary if you need help with a word.

<u>Example:</u>   Be not apt to relate News if you know not the truth thereof.

<u>Answer:</u>   Don't spread gossip.

1.   Shift not yourself in the Sight of others nor Gnaw your nails.

2.   Shew not yourself glad at the Misfortune of another though he were your enemy.

3.   When a man does all he can though it Succeeds not well blame not him that did it.

4.   Wherein you reprove Another be unblameable yourself; for example is more prevalent than Precepts.

5.   Be not hasty to beleive flying Reports to the Disparagement of any.

6.   Associate yourself with Men of good Quality if you Esteem your own Reputation; for 'tis better to be alone than in bad Company.

7.   Give not Advice without being Ask'd & when desired do it briefly.

8.   Keep your Fingers clean & when foul wipe them on a Corner of your Table Napkin.

9.   Put not another bit into your Mouth til the former be Swallowed let not your Morsels be too big for the Gowls [jowls].

10.   Drink not nor talk with your mouth full.

11.   Cleanse not your teeth with the Table Cloth, Napkin, Fork, or Knife but if Others do it let it be done wt. a Pick Tooth.

12.   If others talk at Table be attentive but talk not with Meat in your Mouth.

Name: _____ Date: _____

Interview a Colonist

You are a reporter for an English newspaper in 1650. Your boss sent you to the American colonies to write an article about life in the New World.

What is the name, age, and occupation of the person you will interview?

_____

_____

Write 12 questions you might ask that person during an interview.

1. _____

_____

2. _____

_____

3. _____

_____

4. _____

_____

5. _____

_____

6. _____

_____

7. _____

_____

8. _____

_____

9. _____

_____

10. _____

_____

11. _____

_____

12. _____

_____

Name: _____ Date: _____

Colonial Scavenger Hunt

To complete this scavenger hunt, use the Internet and other reference materials to find the answers.

1. The first book of poetry in America was written by a woman. It was published in England in 1650. Who was she? _____

2. In 1639, the first woman lawyer in the colonies requested the right to vote. She was refused, even though she met the requirements of owning land. Who was she?

    _____

3. In 1639, the first post office in the colonies was operated out of the home of Richard Fairbanks. He charged one penny for each letter. In what city did he live?

    _____

4. In 1652, the first colonial mint opened in Boston, Massachusetts. Although it was against the law for colonists to make their own money, this silversmith minted a new coin called the pine tree shilling. What was his name? _____

5. Although best known for founding the colony of Rhode Island, this man also compiled the first Native American dictionary. Who was he? _____

6. This famous university, founded in 1701 in Killingsworth, Connecticut, was first called the Collegiate School. In 1745, the school moved to New Haven, Connecticut, and was renamed. What is the name of that university? _____

7. *Poor Richard's Almanack* was first published in Philadelphia, Pennsylvania, in 1732. Who was the publisher? _____

8. According to legend, this famous princess saved Captain John Smith from death in Jamestown, Virginia. Who was she? _____

9. Of the first five presidents of the United States, four were born in Virginia. Which one was born in Massachusetts? _____

10. This First Lady, born in 1768 in North Carolina, was raised as a Quaker. Who was she?

    _____

Name: _____ Date: _____

Colonial Word Search

Look up, down, backward, forward, and diagonally to find the 40 words hidden in the puzzle.

```
J T H G I R W N I A W U J S J O J U R J H F F I
K P R E K A M E O H S D H T I M S N I T Q H I M
Y D H A N L O W G N I T L I U Q L H V S Q I G M
B U T T E R K J A Z S N I B A C G O L J H I A E
A T T E L E Y Q W H E E L W R I G H T K K R Z G
W H Y D G F S B G N I N N I P S Y S R T W P T T
C D N K E T T L E S B L O T G Y L L E J S O D O
H I X N E B Q J S C O L O N I S T S F S R F O O
Q O P A E W T A P P R E N T I C E U F P K B I L
O C R S W V G Q K I R P N X A S A B Y I N L B S
J A M S F Y A C C Z L E F D G S C C J C R P A T
N U G F E K O E N O G J Q N E Z O H O E G F R R
A G S O K S K P W H Q Q I L R R T Q O S L U R K
E Q M N F H P A K A I M D R N E M K N O Y F E I
C T M E A A E D N X R N J H E T L I T O L K L T
B A X P O S J G B A A N U T C P U P L L P Q S C
A O L S E P I W F C P S T S I H O L M L G V Z H
R E C Y C L E T V Z K R V S U P U O L A E Z V E
X F L Q G K Q J R S K S A Y U F Q R C M S R T N
H X O J H A N S Y A N E D O N V S Q N Q B R X Y
M U L L L K M T B N L E E T S E I N O L O C H N
U H N L A F E E K S D E X X B G S V F D G J M G
V X Z T O V G V S L D O V O G R I S T M I L L J
T O K T G J C T H H T I M S K C A L B I L W P D
```

APPRENTICE	CORNHUSKS	KITCHEN	SOAP
ARTISANS	EGGS	LOG CABINS	SPICES
BARRELS	FARMING	MILLER	SPINNING
BLACKSMITH	GAMES	OXEN	TINSMITH
BUTTER	GRISTMILL	PLOW	TOOLS
CANDLES	HORSES	QUILTING	TOYS
CHURN	HUNT	RECYCLE	WAINWRIGHT
COLONIES	JAM	SAMPLER	WEAVE
COLONISTS	JELLY	SCHOOL	WHEELWRIGHT
COOPER	KETTLES	SHOEMAKER	WOOL

58

Report on a Colonist

Learn more about a person who was important during the colonial period of American history. Select one of the people listed below for a three- to five-page report. Use the Internet and other reference sources. Add illustrations.

Peter Stuyvesant

Abigail Adams
Ann Austin
John Billington
William Bradford
Anne Bradstreet
Margaret Brent
George Calvert
Rev. John Elliot
Mary Fisher
Benjamin Franklin
Patrick Henry
Thomas Hooker
John Hull
Anne Hutchinson
Margaret Jones
Captain William Kidd
Cotton Mather
Increase Mather
Peter Minuit
James Ogelthorpe
William Penn
Pocahontas
Chief Powhatan
Sir Walter Raleigh
Paul Revere
John Rolfe
Betsy Ross
Captain John Smith
Squanto
Myles Standish
Peter Stuyvesant
Roger Williams
Samuel Winslow
John Winthrop

Abigail Adams

Betsy Ross

Roger Williams

Suggested Reading

The American Girls Collection:
- *Felicity's Cook Book*
- *Felicity's Craft Book*
- *Welcome to Felicity's World: Growing Up in Colonial America*

Colonial Kids: An Activity Guide to Life in the New World by Laurie Carlson

Colonial Americans and Colonial American Craftsmen series by Leonard Everett Fisher:
- *The Peddlers*
- *The Doctors*
- *The Homemakers*
- *The Silversmiths*
- *The Glassmakers*
- *The Blacksmiths*
- *The Papermakers*
- *The Schoolmasters*
- *The Tanners*
- *The Architects*
- *The Potters*
- *The Shipbuilders*
- *The Hatters*
- *The Wigmakers*
- *The Printers*
- *The Cabinetmakers*
- *The Shoemakers*
- *The Weavers*
- *The Limners*

The Patchwork Quilt by Valerie Flourney

Books by Bobbie Kalman:
- *Colonial Crafts*
- *The Gristmill*
- *The Kitchen*
- *Visiting a Village*
- *Early Schools*
- *Home Crafts*
- *Tools and Gadgets*

Books by Deborah Kent:
- *African-Americans in the Thirteen Colonies*
- *In the Middle Colonies (How We Lived)*
- *In the Southern Colonies (How We Lived)*

The New Americans: Colonial Times 1620 - 1689 by Betsy Maestro

If You Had Lived in Colonial Times by Ann McGovern

The Explorers and Settlers: A Sourcebook on Colonial America by Carter Smith

Books by Kate Waters:
- *Sarah Morton's Day: A Day in the Life of a Pilgrim Girl*
- *Samuel Eaton's Day: A Day in the Life of a Pilgrim Boy*

Answer Keys

Exploring a New World (page 3)
1. Yes
2. Ferdinand Magellan
3. Answers will vary.

Colonizing the New World (page 4)
1. Pedro Menendez
2. *Canada* means "village."
   Quebec means "the place where the river narrows."
3. Wilmington

Where Were the First Colonies? (page 7)
Teacher Check Map
1. Portsmouth, New Hampshire
2. Salem, Massachusetts
3. Boston, Massachusetts
4. Plymouth, Massachusetts
5. Providence, Rhode Island
6. Hartford, Connecticut
7. Albany, New York
8. New York, New York
9. Philadelphia, Pennsylvania
10. Baltimore, Maryland
11. Williamsburg, Virginia
12. Norfolk, Virginia
13. Charleston, South Carolina
14. Savannah, Georgia
15. Saint Augustine, Florida

Building a Log Cabin (page 8)
1. 28 logs
2. They would let in too much cold air, rain, etc.

Baking Bread (page 11)
1. 40 cups
2. To mix and work (dough) into a pliable mass by folding over, pressing, and squeezing, usually with the hands

Colonial Tools (page 14)
1. H   spider
2. C   iron
3. D   warming pan
4. A   goffer
5. G   hay fork
6. I   tongs
7. B   drawknife
8. E   hackle
9. J   ruggle
10. F   rug beater

What's for Dinner? (page 16)
1. Possible answers: bread, pancakes, scrambled or fried eggs, butter, buttermilk, biscuits, pie crust, dumplings
2. Possible answers: deer, turkeys, pheasants, squirrels, rabbits, possums, ducks, fish, raccoons, bear, quail
3. Honey, maple syrup, berries, nuts, chives, mushrooms, acorns
4. Peas, corn, carrots, potatoes, beets, turnips, cabbage, beans, onions, pumpkins

Soapmaking (page 20)
2. lye, grease (tallow), and water
3. Soapmaking was messy and smelled bad.
4. Lye can burn skin, eyes, or lungs. It is poisonous if swallowed.

From Wool to Clothing (page 23)
1. The sheep need the wool to stay warm during the winter.
4. The cloth was made at home from yarn spun on a spinning wheel.
5.
   3 spin wool into yarn
   1 shear sheep
   5 dye, cut, and sew clothes
   2 clean wool
   4 weave yarn into cloth

Cornhusk Dolls (page 30)
1. Corn was unknown in Europe before people began settling in the New World.

Livestock (page 33)
1. They could pull plows and harrows, pull wagons and carriages, provide power for mills, pull boats along canals, and people could ride horses.
2. They were the main animal used for riding and pulling wagons and carriages. There were no automobiles then.
3. Pigs (pork): ham, roast, chops, ribs, bacon, pig's feet, sausage, organ meats
   Cows (beef): steaks, roast, stew meat, ribs, organ meats
   Sheep (lamb): chops, roast, leg of lamb
   Geese and chickens: roasted, baked, or fried; eggs
4. Pigs: hides for leather, lard for cooking
   Cows: hides for leather; tallow for candles and soap; gelatin or glue from hooves, hides, and bones
   Sheep: wool, hide for parchment and leather
   Geese and chickens: feathers for stuffing and quill pens

Answer Keys

5. As a guard dog, to warn of strangers, as a herding dog, to keep pests away
6. Answers will vary.

Trading for Goods and Services (page 34)

Answers will vary, but try to make sure the values are approximately equal.

Coopers (page 38)

1. A small wooden pail with one stave extended above the rim to serve as a handle
3. A winch, especially a simple one worked by a crank

Cabinetmakers (page 39)

1. A machine for shaping an article of wood by holding and turning it rapidly against the edge of a cutting or abrading tool
2. To make table and chair legs, spindles, balusters for stairways, spokes for wheels, etc.

Wheelwrights (page 40)

1. A. iron ring   C. spoke
   B. rim   D. hub

2. Wainwrights made wagons.
3. They were all craftspeople who worked with wood.

Blacksmiths (page 41)

2. That can be hammered, pounded, or pressed into various shapes without breaking
3. Shoe horses

Leatherworkers (page 44)

1. The leather straps and metal pieces by which a horse, mule, etc., is fastened to a vehicle, plow, or load
3. The shoemaker could make a standard shoe for each size and not have to worry about different patterns for different feet.

Papermakers (page 45)

Answers will vary. Possible answers are given.
1. Tree bark, cloth, parchment, the ground, quill and ink, charcoal stick, pencil, stick
2. The skin of an animal, usually a sheep or goat, prepared as a surface on which to write or paint

Life in a Colonial Village (page 50)

3. Four hours
4. Eight hours
5. Silver, pewter, or tinware, pottery, leather goods, furniture, etc.

6. Milling grain, doctor, lawyer, horse shoeing, carpentry, etc.
7. Mill, stable, church, general store, etc.

Community Spirit (page 51)

1. All the people living in a particular district, city, etc.
2. The feeling that everyone in the community should work together for the good of all

Colonial Education (page 53)

2. Mathematics or math
4. A hard, fine-grained, metamorphic rock that cleaves naturally into thin, smooth-surfaced layers; it is used as a tablet for writing on with chalk

Rules of Civility & Decent Behaviour in Company and Conversation (page 55)

Answers will vary. Accept answers that convey the general meaning of the original.

Colonial Scavenger Hunt (page 57)

1. Anne Bradstreet
2. Margaret Brent
3. Boston
4. John Hull
5. Roger Williams
6. Yale University
7. Benjamin Franklin
8. Pocahontas
9. John Adams
10. Dolley Madison

Colonial Word Search (page 58)

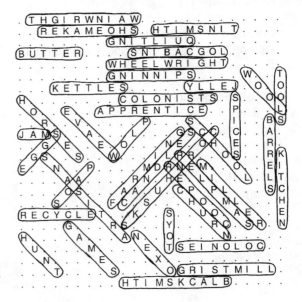